To my mother who instilled that beauty is about respecting yourself, being kind to others, and appreciating what you have.

To my daughter Olivia—you are a gift. May I be able to teach you as much as Grandma Nunu taught me. Stay joyful, sweet, and loving. Most importantly, keep smiling—if you feel happiness in your heart, beauty will always radiate.

This book belongs to:

Meggenveller

One morning, Penny woke up after a long night of sleep.
It was time to get ready for school.

She was excited to see her friends so she eagerly jumped
out of bed to get ready for her day.

But, when she looked in the mirror, her excitement turned into sadness.

Penny noticed her hair was a mess,

her feathers were all rumpled,

and her face was missing that special glow.

So, she started to comb her hair,

iron her feathers,

and wash her face,

but nothing helped.

Penny's mother said, "Hi beautiful, I made your
favorite breakfast—pancakes with powdered sugar."
But, Penny just frowned.

"Mommy, I'm not beautiful—my hair is a mess, my feathers are all rumpled, and my face is missing that glow."

"Penny, you know beauty is not about how you look on the outside, it's about how you feel on the inside. And, you are beautiful because you have happiness in your heart."

On her way to school, Penny thought about
her mother's words.

She had loving parents,

kind friends,

delicious food to eat,

great books to read,

and a house filled with lots of fun and laughter.

And, all of a sudden she started smiling
and feeling happy again.

She proudly walked into school that day

and saw her friends waiting for her.

Coco said, "Penny, there's something different about you."

And, Penny started to frown again thinking about
what a mess she was.

"Yeah," said Shelly, "You look...so...

beautiful."

And, Penny finally understood her mother's words.

Beauty is not about how you look;
it's all about how you feel.

And, on this day,

Penny felt like the most beautiful peacock in the world.

About the Author

This is Roopa Weber's first children's book. She was inspired by the peacock, which grazed in India, where her parents were raised, and in Africa, where she was born. Growing up, the peacock feather symbolized good luck and so she hopes its good fortune, richness, and splendor will always follow her daughter.

Roopa resides in Chicago, Illinois with her loving husband and daughter. The trio shouts that life is beautiful. Embrace every moment.

About the Illustrator

Manda Satkoski-Szewczyk is a designer and illustrator living in Valparaiso, Indiana. She would like to thank her wonderful husband and family for all of their support while she worked on this book. She would especially like to thank her mom for a lifetime of encouragement, advice, and unconditional love: Mom, I love you.

Karma Kollection LLC

Chicago, IL

Cover art and illustrations by Manda Szewczyk

Copyright © 2013 by Karma Kollection LLC

All rights reserved

MessyPenny.com

facebook.com/PennyThePeacock

twitter.com/RoopaWeber

CPSIA information can be obtained
at www.ICGtesting.com
Printed in the USA
LVIC05n2333041114
412083LV00006B/30